Eight Hands Round

A Patchwork Alphabet

by ANN WHITFORD PAUL ■ *illustrated by* JEANETTE WINTER

HarperCollins*Publishers*

For Mom and Dad,

with love

A.W.P.

In memory of

Etta Winter

J.W.

EIGHT HANDS ROUND: *A Patchwork Alphabet*
Text copyright © 1991 by Ann Whitford Paul
Illustrations copyright © 1991 by Jeanette Winter
Manufactured in China. All rights reserved.

Library of Congress Cataloging-in-Publication Data
Paul, Ann Whitford.
    Eight hands round: a patchwork alphabet / by Ann Whitford Paul ; illustrated by
Jeanette Winter.
        p.   cm.
    Summary: Introduces the letters of the alphabet with names of early American
patchwork quilt patterns and explains the origins of the designs by describing the
activity or occupation they derive from.
    ISBN 0-06-024689-8. — ISBN 0-06-024704-5 (lib. bdg.)
    ISBN 0-06-443464-8 (pbk.)
    1. Quilting—United States—Patterns—Juvenile literature.   2. Patchwork—
United States—Patterns—Juvenile literature.   [1. Quilting.   2. Patchwork.   3.
Alphabet.]   I. Winter, Jeanette, ill.   II. Title.
TT835.P386   1991   88-745
746.9'7'0973—dc19   CIP
[E]   AC

*P*atchwork is pieces of fabric cut into different shapes and sewn together into patterns. During the first one hundred years after the signing of the Declaration of Independence, many women and girls—and even a few men and boys—sewed patchwork.

Patchwork was important because no one could afford to waste good fabrics. At one time women wove all their fabrics at home. Even when machines and factories began to produce fabric, it was expensive and difficult to get.

With patchwork, people could use the tiny scraps left over from the dresses and shirts they had sewn. They could also re-use fabric, cut into small pieces, from outgrown or worn-out clothing.

The patchwork pieces were sewn together by hand. It took many, many hours. To make those hours pass more quickly, women sometimes invited friends to sew with them.

When they finished, they usually made the patchwork into warm quilts for their beds. Sometimes they gave their quilts as gifts to a new bride, a new baby, or to a good friend who was moving away. These patchwork quilts added welcome color to homes that were often without any other decoration.

Where did people get their ideas for the designs and names of patchwork patterns? Some came from tools they used or toys children played with. Others came from plants, animals, or stars. Sometimes a design was made up and then named after a special event, an important person, or a story in the Bible.

Not everyone who sewed patchwork made up new patterns. Some just used patterns they had seen before. But because each person used her own combination of fabrics and colors, no two patchworks were the same.

Old patchwork patterns with their beautiful designs and interesting names can tell us how people lived when our country was still young and growing.

$\mathcal{A}$nvil

Two hundred years ago most towns had a blacksmith. An anvil always sat on a flat stump in his shop. The blacksmith softened pieces of iron in a huge fire. Then, with long tongs, he removed the iron from the fire and placed it on his anvil. When the blacksmith wanted to make the iron flat, he hammered it on the flat part of the anvil. When he wanted the iron curved, he hammered it around the pointed part of the anvil. The blacksmith made many useful things out of iron. He made hatchets, hoes, and shoes for horses. Maybe a blacksmith, or his wife, thought up this pattern. Or maybe the idea came to a customer waiting patiently in his shop on a cold winter afternoon.

Buggy Wheel

Going from one place to another usually meant walking, riding a horse, or sitting in a buggy pulled by a horse. A buggy was a wooden seat on a wooden platform over wooden wheels. Depending on the weather, the buggy ride could be wet, hot, or chilly. It was always bumpy and slow. Buggies rarely traveled over twenty miles in one day. Perhaps the person who thought up this pattern did so while taking a trip in a buggy.

Churn Dash

The family cow provided the milk that was used to make butter. Usually it was the woman's job to milk the cow and pour the cream that rose to the top of the pail into a thin wooden barrel called a churn. Then she rolled the pole sticking out of the churn back and forth between her hands. The rolling turned the dash, which was the wooden piece shaped like this pattern, at the other end of the pole. The dash whipped the cream until it separated into butter. Maybe the idea for this pattern came to someone while churning.

Does and Darts

A doe is a female deer. Deer were hunted for their tasty meat. They were also hunted for their hides, which were used to make sturdy pants and jackets for men and boys. White settlers usually hunted for deer with guns while Indians used guns, darts, or arrows shot from bows. When settlers killed more deer than they needed, they went to a trading post and traded the extra hides for goods such as knives and kettles. Sometimes they traded for brightly colored cloth so their wives, or daughters, could sew more patchwork.

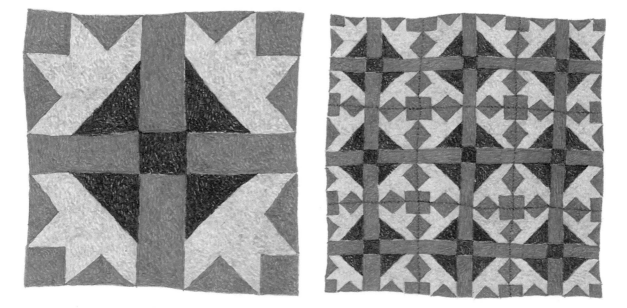

Eight Hands Round

Often when a woman finished a large patchwork, she invited her friends to a quilting party. The women sat around a wooden frame with two layers of cloth stretched across it. The patchwork was placed on top. They sewed these materials together with tiny stitches, making a quilt. When they finished, their husbands joined them for supper. After eating, someone picked up a fiddle, a caller hollered, "Grab your partner," and four couples hurried to form a square. They clapped their hands and stamped their feet. And when the caller said, "Eight hands round," they all joined hands in a circle.

Flying Geese

People raised geese for their eggs, meat, and feathers. It was the woman's job to pluck the goose. She had to wear a cap to keep the feathers from flying into her hair and she put a stocking, or a special basket, over the goose's head to prevent it from biting her. Maybe the person who made up this pattern was thanking her goose for giving its soft downy feathers for pillows and its pointed quills for writing pens.

Grandmother's Fan

Sometimes when a woman went out on a summer night, she carried a fan. Fans were made of feathers, lace, silk, or a specially treated sheepskin called parchment. The handles were made of carved ivory, tortoiseshell, or wood. To cool herself, the woman spread the fan out wide and fluttered it back and forth in front of her face. Then she folded the fan and held it until she was warm again. It's possible a woman first sewed this pattern by copying the shape of her grandmother's fan.

Honeycomb

In the early years of independence, many people raised bees in hives made of straw or the hollow section of a tree. When it was time to gather the honey, they set rags on fire to smoke the bees out of the hive. Then it was safe to cut away the honeycombs and separate the honey from the comb with a linen strainer. People used honey in cakes and to sweeten their fruit and puddings. But most often—like people today—they loved honey, thickly spread, on bread.

Indian Hatchet

When Indians fought or hunted, they often used a hatchet called a tomahawk. Indians made their hatchets out of wood and stone, or they traded with white settlers for the iron ones blacksmiths made. Sometimes Indians decorated their hatchets with feathers, quills, and paint, and used them in a dance. Perhaps someone who saw an Indian dance with his hatchet first made up this pattern.

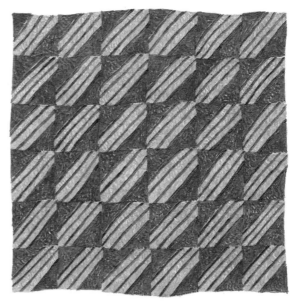

Jacob's Ladder

The story of Jacob comes from the Old Testament of the Bible. Jacob left his father's home. At night he laid his head on a stone to sleep and dreamed of a ladder reaching to heaven. In his dream, God told Jacob that he and his children could have the land he was sleeping on. God promised to always be with Jacob's children even though they might travel long distances. A quilt made from this patchwork pattern must have comforted those settlers who had to build new homes far away from their families and friends.

*K*ite's Tail

A hundred years ago or more, most children made their own kites. Sometimes their parents helped them. They sewed or glued thin paper or cloth onto a stick frame. Small pieces of brightly colored paper or cloth worked perfectly for the kite's tail. Then all they needed was a long cord and a good strong wind. Perhaps a boy or his sister thought up this pattern while flying a kite across a meadow.

Log Cabin

In the early 1800s a man needed two strong arms, an ax, and lots of tall trees to build a log cabin. First he chopped down the trees. Then he removed the branches and cut the logs into proper lengths. He made a notch at each end of the logs so they would fit neatly. Then he stacked them one on top of another. In this patchwork pattern, the strips of cloth are stacked like the logs of a cabin.

$\mathcal{M}$aple Leaf

At the end of winter, when warmer days started the sap flowing in the maple trees, fathers and sons cut notches in the trunks. They placed a spout in each notch so the sap could drip into wooden troughs. Then they cooked the sap in a huge pot over a roaring fire until it thickened into syrup. Often they invited their neighbors to a party. Everyone had a good time tasting the new syrup and making maple-sugar candy in the snow.

 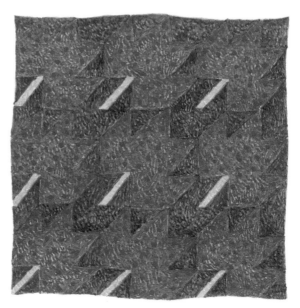

Necktie

When boys and their fathers went to town, to church, or to a party, they usually wore neckties tied in bows. Some of the bows were big and fluffy. Some were small and thin. Men wore their neckties over shirts with collars that occasionally came up to their chins. Perhaps the idea for this pattern came to a young man learning to make a bow with his necktie.

O ld Tippecanoe

Old Tippecanoe was the nickname of our ninth president, William Henry Harrison. In the early 1800s, a Shawnee Indian named Tecumseh urged several Indian tribes to join together to fight for lands they felt had been taken from them. Harrison, who was then a general, led troops that attacked and defeated these Indians at the Tippecanoe River in Indiana. Probably the person who named this pattern supported Harrison when he later ran for president.

Postage Stamp

Long ago letters were not delivered to homes, nor did mail come every day. People had to go to the post office the day the letters were due and wait in long lines for them to be sorted. Usually they had to pay for each letter they received. But after 1847, a stamp stuck on the letter showed that the sender had paid the postage. This pattern made good use of tiny pieces of fabric. It also reminded people of the letters they hoped to receive from faraway family and friends.

Queen Charlotte's Crown

People came from all over to live in America. Some came from Asia and Africa. Most came from Europe, especially England. Charlotte, wife of George III, was the queen of England at the time of the signing of the Declaration of Independence and the Revolutionary War. Possibly an immigrant thought of this pattern while standing on the ship's deck watching England disappear on the horizon.

Rocky Road to Kansas

The roads to Kansas, and to almost everywhere, were rocky. Many were just narrow paths through the woods. For a man alone on his horse, that was good enough. But for a family in a buggy filled with belongings, it was not. Often they had to stop and cut down trees to widen the path. When they came to a swamp, they had to lay tree trunks side by side in order to cross it. Maybe a woman thought up this pattern after helping change a path into a road.

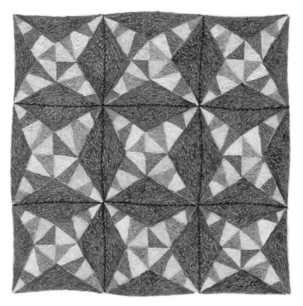

Storm at Sea

During a storm at sea, gusty winds and crashing waves tossed ships about until the sailors had no idea how to reach safe harbor. It was hard to see through the darkness and slanting rains, and sometimes their ships crashed into the jagged rocks near shore. Lighthouses were built where the coast was most dangerous. The keeper kept a bright flame burning high in the tower, and when seamen saw the light, they knew to steer their ships away. Perhaps the daughter of a lighthouse keeper first sewed this pattern during a storm at sea.

Tobacco Leaves

Tobacco was grown in the South on large farms called plantations. Black slaves—some of them young children—worked in the tobacco fields planting seeds, pulling weeds, and killing worms that ate the crop. They also picked the leaves at harvesttime and hung them to dry in special barns. Possibly a slave, exhausted from working many hours in a tobacco field, thought up this pattern.

Underground Railroad

The Underground Railroad was not a railroad and it was not underground. It was a group of people helping southern blacks escape slavery. The runaway slaves had to travel long distances, often alone and at night, because it was against the law in the South to escape. Underground Railroad people gave the runaways food, fresh clothes, and a safe place to sleep. Then they directed them to another Underground Railroad person farther north where they could be safe. Perhaps the first person to sew this pattern was a black woman who, with the help of the Underground Railroad, escaped slavery and became a free person.

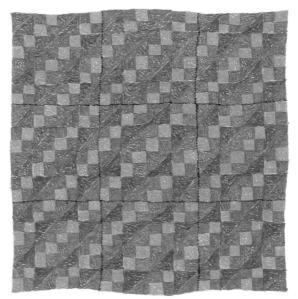

Variable Star

Riding a horse or bouncing along in a buggy or covered wagon was slow and the distance between towns was great. Houses were usually far apart, separated by huge fields, forests, or prairies. Often when night came, travelers had no place to sleep but on the hard ground. Perhaps one of these weary travelers came, at last, to a house and was invited inside by the family. Maybe he thought up this pattern because he was so happy to sleep under a roof instead of the stars.

Windmill

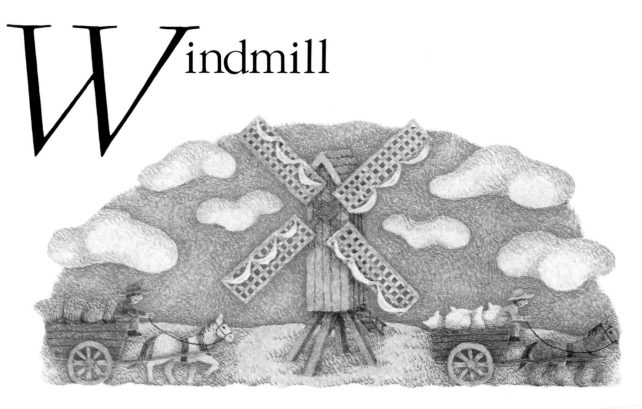

Many towns along the East Coast had windmills that looked like tall, thin houses standing on posts. Farmers placed their wheat between two large stones inside the house. When the wind blew the vanes attached to the outside of the house around and around, the millstones rubbed against each other, grinding the wheat into flour. Farmers paid the man who ran the mill with part of their freshly ground flour. They took the rest home where the women used it to make bread and biscuits and cakes.

X

Because many towns did not have schools, some people never learned to read or write even their own name. But when a person bought land, borrowed money, or went to court, the law said he had to sign his name to an official paper. If a man could not write, he would have someone else do it for him, leaving a space between his first and last names. Then he would make an *X* in that space. The *X* was called his mark and it stood for his name. Possibly the person who made up this pattern was "signing" her patchwork.

Yankee Puzzle

People who live in New England are called Yankees. A hundred years ago or more, many Yankees enjoyed playing with a puzzle that had seven small pieces—five triangles, one square, and one rhomboid—made of ivory, wood, or pasteboard. The object was to arrange the pieces into different designs. People made vases, daggers, or boats. They also made flowers, houses, or chairs. Sometimes they made up their own designs, just like the person who made up this patchwork pattern.

Zigzag

This pattern was sometimes called Streak of Lightning. People who lived on the plains were especially afraid of lightning because during a hot summer, it could set the dry grass on fire. A strong wind could spread the fire, threatening their homes, their animals, and their crops. The whole family helped fight such a fire. They used wet blankets and pails filled with water from a well or a nearby stream. Maybe a woman sewed this pattern so she would not forget how hard everyone once worked to save her home from a lightning fire.

Now you know twenty-six different patchwork patterns. There are thousands more. Look for them in books, in museums, or in stores. See what they can tell you about life during the time the patchwork was sewn.